Growing Readers

Purchased with Smart Start Funds

Thoughts and Feelings

Thoughts and Feelings

I'm Sorry

Written by Susan Riley
Photos by David M. Budd

The Child's World®, Inc.

Published by The Child's World®, Inc.

Design and Production:
The Creative Spark, San Juan Capistrano, CA

Photos: © 1998 David M. Budd Photography

Library of Congress Cataloging-in-Publication Data

Riley, Susan, 1946–
    I'm Sorry / by Susan Riley.
        p. cm. — (Thoughts and feelings)
    Includes bibliographical references (p.).
    Summary: Identifies occasions when one may "feel sorry," such as being
late, illness, and spilling milk.
    ISBN 1-56766-675-2 (alk. paper)
    1. Sadness Juvenile literature. 2. Regret Juvenile literature. [1. Conduct
of life.]   I. Title. II. Series.
BF575.G7R55   1999
395.1'22—dc21
                                                                99-22905
                                                                   CIP

I didn't make it.
It's past time for our date.

I'm sorry to keep
you waiting.
Sorry to be so late.

9

Here I come now
as fast as I can.

I'm sorry, I'm sorry.
I'll say it again.

Have you ever been sorry for something you've done?
Or have you ever felt sorry for anyone?

I feel sorry for people
when they are sick.
I say, "Sorry you're sick.
Get well quick."

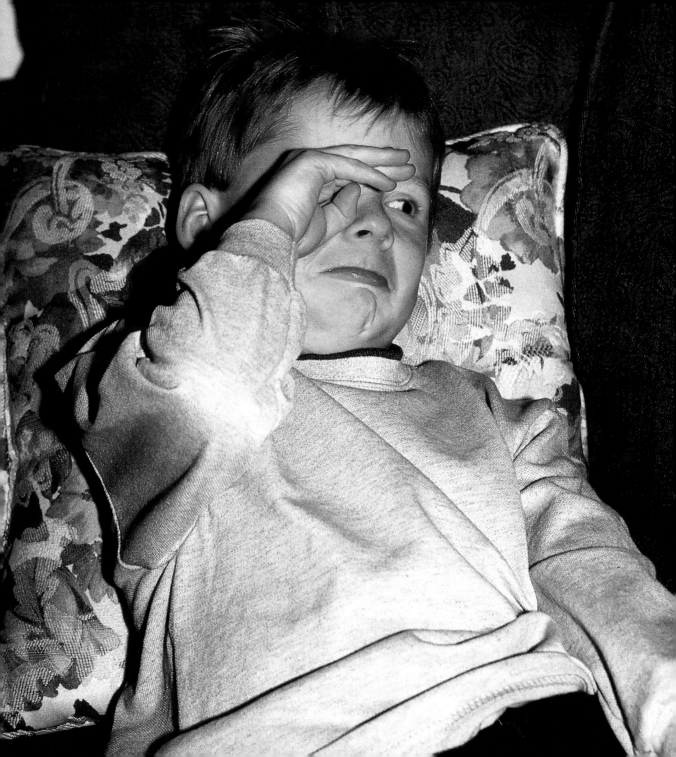

I feel sorry for my brother
whenever he cries.

I give him a hug
and wipe his eyes.

And sometimes I'm sorry
for things that I do.
I say, "I'm sorry I did that.
I didn't mean to."

If I spill my milk

22

or break a glass,

23

or if I'm a little bit late for my class.

I always say, "I'm sorry."
I really do.

"I'm sorry" means,
"I'll try to do better," too.   27

28

Remember to say
you're sorry—
just like me.

Saying **SORRY**

makes everyone
feel better, you see.

For Further Information and Reading

Books

Buehner, Caralyn. *I Did It, I'm Sorry.* New York: Dial Books, 1998.

Furtado, Jo. *I'm Sorry, Miss Folio!* Brooklyn, NY: Kane/Miller Books, 1992.

Joslin, Sesyle. *What Do You Say, Dear?* New York: Harper Collins, 1987.

Ziegler, Sandra. *The Child's World® of Manners.* Chanhassen, MN: The Child's World, 1997.

Web Sites

For more information about thoughts and feelings:
http://www.kidshealth.org/kid/feeling/

Top Seven Manners Kids Should Know:
http://www.lifetimetv.com/parenting/kidman.html

Fairy tales and stories about thoughts and feelings from all over the world: http://www.familyinternet.com/StoryGrowby/